MAGNETIC ATTRACTION

Cover art and illustrations
by
Susan Netherwood

MAGNETIC ATTRACTION

The Secret to Compatibility
between
the 12 Zodiac Signs

by
Maggie Bird

Printed in the United States of America

ISBN 978-0-615-75366-9

Published by:

CP

cunningham press

CONTENTS

INTRODUCTION

The *secret to compatibility in love* can be found in a little used fact listed in the astrological descriptions of the twelve zodiac signs. All of the zodiac signs have been given a list of attributes and keywords that categorize and describe each sign. Take a look at the first sign of the zodiac, Aries. Aries is described as a cardinal sign, a fire sign, ruled by the planet Mars, has a ram as its symbol and is associated with the head, face, and muscles. Then, lastly it mentions that it is said to have a positive polarity designation. This designation of either positive or negative "polarity" is what has been overlooked for so long in regard to love and compatibility.

1

The study of Astrology compatibility is called Synastry and it has been baffling astrologers for years. The prevailing thought in Astrology books today is that the fire and air signs would be a good match for each other and that the water and earth signs would also make a good match.

The fact is that the fire and air signs are both designated as positively charged and are therefore the "same" in respect to polarity. The water and the earth signs are both designated as negatively charged and are also the "same." Two of the same do not make a match. For a match to work, one of each polarity is needed. One positive and one negative is necessary for a match to be successful...

...(or even have a chance to be successful)... just because you meet someone that is the proper polarity for you, this doesn't mean that this is the person for you. It only means that this person has the correct polarity for you.

This formula of needing one plus and one minus can be seen in the natural order of nature. This is the pairing of a male (positive) and a female (negative) that come together "to work" if you will, and reproduce, which is the function that makes "life" itself go on.

This book is dedicated to making the polarity of the twelve Astrology signs common knowledge. For those seeking partnerships, this book declares that six of the Astrology signs are designated as positively charged and the other six Astrology signs are designated as negatively charged. I recommend the reader to consider this advice before getting married and making a family with someone that has the same polarity as yourself.

the positively charged signs (fire & air):

Aries	3/21 to 4/19
Gemini	5/21 to 6/20
Leo	7/23 to 8/22
Libra	9/23 to 10/22
Sagittarius	11/22 to 12/21
Aquarius	1/20 to 2/18

the negatively charged signs (water & earth):

Taurus	4/20 to 5/20
Cancer	6/21 to 7/22
Virgo	8/23 to 9/22
Scorpio	10/23 to 11/21
Capricorn	12/22 to 1/19
Pisces	2/19 to 3/20

If your sign or birthday falls in the first group of positively charged signs, you are compatible with all the signs listed in the second group of negatively charged signs. If your sign or birthday is in the second group of negatively charged signs, you are compatible with all the signs listed in the top group of positively charged signs. You are not compatible (regarding love and sex) with the signs that are in the same group as yourself.

The exact dates and time when the Astrology signs begin and end, vary each year due to the adding of a day, every four years, for leap year. People born on the cusp between signs, need to know their exact time of birth, in order to find out which sign they were born under. This can be accomplished by consulting an Astrologer or an ephemeris, a reference book that details this information. There are websites on the Internet that will do a natal chart for free.

ASTROLOGY 101

Astrology is one of the first intellectual pursuits that early man found interesting. Moon phases drawn on cave walls have been recorded as far back as 25,000 years ago. The word Astrology from early Latin: "astrologia" means 'account of the stars.' Astrology is a study of the celestial bodies in our solar system and how their position and motion can relate to the lives of people on the earth.

The study of Astrology is so old, it came before man knew that the Earth was round. Today Astrology remains a current interest for people and it can be found in books, newspapers, magazines and on the Internet. The signs and symbols of the planets, and the twelve zodiac signs are still listed in dictionaries and almanacs.

The moment that a person is born into the world is the basis for a natal horoscope. The Sun, Moon and planets are each in a specific place in the sky and their exact position at the time and location of your birth becomes your natal Astrology chart. This is your horoscope which is a picture of the sky at the moment you were born.

Astrology can be thought of in 2 parts. The first is the natal chart which is the picture of the sky when you were born and all the descriptions of what is found there. Then, as you age, day by day, the planets continue to move in their orbits, and their mathematical relationship (aspects or angles) to the place where the planets were on your birth day is the other part of Astrology, which people associate with prediction.

In Astrology, the sky is divided up into twelve sections and each of these areas correspond with one of the zodiac signs. Each day at sunrise, a new day begins and the sun is one degree further along a celestial clock. The first day of spring is March 21st and at sunrise, the "Sun" (or someone's birthday) is coming across the horizon as the first degree of Aries.

March 21st begins the 30 days that come over the horizon at sunrise called Aries. Next comes Taurus, then Gemini, etc. Cancer is the first sign of summer and it starts to come over the horizon at sunrise on June 21st. At any given time, when a particular section of sky is coming over the horizon at sunrise, that denotes an Astrology sign.

If you were born in Atlantic City, NJ, USA on July 25 at 11 AM, you would be a Leo with Libra rising. The time of year makes you a Leo because Leo is coming over the horizon at sunrise. But, because you were born at 11 AM, the Sun was higher in the sky and by then Libra was coming over the horizon which gives you Libra rising. Horoscopes in newspapers and magazines reference the rising sign at sunrise. So, this Leo should be reading Libra to get a correct appraisal of their current horoscope.

Time of day, like 11 AM, is responsible for determining the rising sign. In Astrology, the rising sign is almost as important as the "Sun sign" and is often associated with a person's physical appearance. The horizon is called the ascendant which is positioned at the beginning of an Astrology chart's first house, said to relate to what one looks like.

The descriptions of a Sun sign (Astrology sign) rely heavily on two sets of categorizations. One is called the Triplicities and this divides the twelve signs into: 3 fire signs, 3 air signs, 3 earth signs and 3 water signs.

The other is the Quadruplicities and that divides the twelve signs into: 4 cardinal signs, 4 fixed signs, and 4 mutable signs. These two sets of categorizations relate to positions on a circle. Astrology is based on a circle, and this circle represents the whole sky going around the earth in one year's time. A circle represents life, the life cycle, along with one year of time.

Each sign of the zodiac has a ruling planet. This planet, or it could be the Sun or the Moon, has keywords that identify and depict the celestial body in a fairly specific way. These descriptions, along with the sign's triplicity and quadruplicity categorization become the main characteristics of each of the twelve zodiac signs.

The planets and the solar system are in constant motion, all held together by gravitational pull. Astrology describes this activity. This is the "account of the stars," the Earth's yearly calendar.

Through science we know that the universe has certain forces of nature. These are gravity, electromagnetism and the strong and weak forces. In our solar system we have 9 planets along with the Sun and the Moon. These are real time objects that are influenced by the forces of nature. The motion and cycles of these heavenly bodies are predictable, and the regularity of their mathematical occurrences can be found with exactitude in charts in books. There are many varied types of Astrology throughout the world, and throughout history; but the basic ideas of the different versions of Astrology are very similar to each other.

ARIES

Life begins anew on March 21st, the first day of Spring. We notice the grass is starting to green, and the plants and trees are beginning a new cycle of life. Aries is the first sign of the zodiac and like Spring, Aries likes to burst on the scene. Those born in the sign of Aries are loaded with energy and have a fresh, buoyant attitude toward life. This is a fire sign which indicates enthusiasm for life and a cardinal sign, whose natives have the ability to act decisively. Aries is known as an intellectual sign. They like to be first and to dominate in any endeavor they choose to take on.

Aries rules the head and face, muscles and physical strength. A natural sportsman, they often have red hair, or strawberry blond hair, perhaps with freckles, too. In appearance they can be quite adorable to look at. The face and head may have a great drawing power, making you want to look at them. Some have a tall lanky frame and others a small or short muscular body type.

The sign Aries is ruled by the planet Mars. Keywords associated with Mars are excitement, aggression, physical talent, speed and quick motions. These folks may be seen running instead of walking and wonder why others can't keep up to them. Cheerful and openly friendly, the Aries zest for life can be contagious.

The Sun is said to be in its exaltation when in the first sign of Aries. Purity of head and heart, this primal sign has drive and great potential for positive action. The Aries strong suit lies in an ability to initiate activity with great purpose. They are natural leaders and efficient workers. Those born under the sign of Aries are generators of excitement and seek to involve others in their ideas and propel them into activity.

The here and now is what's important to those governed by the ram. They are often impatient and display a zealous devotion to whatever is their current project. Aries likes a challenge and has difficulty accepting defeat. This exemplifies a youthful innocence that always creates initiative with a fresh approach. People born in Aries exhibit forceful directness and originality, traits so necessary at the inception of a task.

Aries characteristics include honesty and self-confidence. Fire signs have a desire to be liked by everyone. "It's all about me" can be said about Aries who can be totally sweet or completely impossible to reason with.

Aries has a sunny disposition with an ardent desire to enjoy life. Fearless and egocentric, Aries people like to be fussed over, admired and treated with great care. Although occasionally lacking in humility and not long on patience, they have great pride and an optimistic point of view. Aries is a joyous, upbeat sign that won't linger long on negativity. Aries are pioneers and crusaders always looking for the next adventure with their natural fire and passion for life.

TAURUS

Venus is the planet of love and rules Taurus, the second sign of the zodiac. At the end of April when the Earth starts to warm and the first flowers begin to bloom, we are reminded of nature's beauty and the rebirth of life. Taurus represents the love of hearth and home, and of our earthy possessions that give us a sense of security in a world of occasional upheaval. Taurus is a fixed, earth sign that confirms the many adjectives through this association that include determination, constancy, persistence and reliability.

Taurus is a lover of life in all senses; a lover of the opposite sex, a lover of the finer things and a lover of peace and harmony. People born under the sign of Taurus are in "whatever their heart's desire" for the long haul and are not apt to change course quickly. They may be calm and quiet but not fragile and have a naturally easy-going manner. Those ruled by the bull make decisions slowly and carefully, and have great strength of character. More often, they prefer to stay at home and enjoy the pleasantries that life has to offer like music, companionship, good food and wine.

Love and sensuality are an important component of the Taurus personality. Venus stands for romance, true love, and tenderness. With the planet Venus as their ruler, Taurus appreciates form and beauty. Taurus loves to love, and be loved. They can be intensely jealous and sometimes regard another person's affections as their property.

Security, both emotionally and materially is foremost in the world of Taurus. A smooth relationship is best for the bull; if you try to make them over, it won't work because they have their own way of doing things and you probably won't be able to change that. Taurus is protective of themselves and of those they love.

Taurus is the strong silent type with tremendous self-control. They are sensible and can carry many a burden without complaint. They have powerful and sensitive natures coupled with a intellectual capacity that is stimulated by art and music. Taurus rules the neck and throat, and many of the world's finest singers are born under the sign of Taurus. Taurus is a natural being, like nature itself. They care about their fellow man and they care for mankind. More a lover than a fighter, Taurus has a social conscience and is a sympathizer toward the weak or needy.

Taurus is a peaceful sign that treasures a harmonious existence. A person of deliberate choices that is solid and steady; not much can disturb their tranquility. The bull will seldom rush forward to interfere with your plans. Taurus is strong willed and will dig their heels in when someone tries to interfere with their vision. They make decisions when they're good and ready.

Taurus is a power sign that makes headway through life with measured slow and steady progress, plodding down its own road toward eventual success. With conscious effort, Taurus takes a deliberate and practical approach to life. They like a tranquil existence and take challenges in stride. Taurus loves their mother, their home and their place on this earth.

18

GEMINI

Gemini is the third sign of the zodiac and is represented by "the twins." Beginning near the end of May, it's a busy time in the solar year when the moderate temperatures of the season propel everyone to get out and about. Mercury, ruler of Gemini, with that winged-footed symbol, finds people moving around and talking to each other. In this mutable air sign, the Spring breeze is full of gnats, mosquitoes, and bees that flit from flower to flower in the repetitious job of pollination.

This is the season of Gemini, governor of speed and communication, the one with the infinite learning capacity, who can barely quench his thirst for knowledge. This intellectual sign has strong mental abilities and likes to acquire and utilize factual information. Known for originality of thought, Gemini is a mental explorer with many interests and lots of ideas.

Gemini's ruling planet, Mercury, travels around the Sun with great speed and completes over 3 orbits in one Earth year. This motion may result in the many associations to Mercury defined by duality or multiples.

The brain, our thinking machine, has two hemispheres. We have 2 hands, 2 arms, 2 ears and 2 eyes, all in their way, a function of communication. Writing, handwriting and words have a pronounced connection to Gemini through the tie-in to the planet Mercury, which is considered an instrument of transmission.

People born under the sign of Gemini are thought to be versatile, display physical agility, and have manual dexterity. Gemini has excellent mental abilities to put ideas together in creation of a plan or project. A sign of many talents, those ruled by Mercury have a clever tongue and fast mind with a gift of words, that can give Gemini an advantage in business or sales. It wouldn't be wise to challenge them in a battle of wits as

Gemini can talk themselves out of anything. A friend to all, this sign is popular and a natural socializer with stimulating conversation.

Gemini can be aloof and impersonal at times. They do not like to be pinned down to any one place for long. They detest routine and resent drudgery. Gemini prefers to keep moving with their typical abundance of nervous energy. They are easily distracted and often arrive late for appointments because of their natural tendency to become side-tracked. The mercurial nature of Gemini demands constant excitement and change. In relationships, they may not always be forthcoming with their true feelings because they themselves change their minds so often.

Mental activity and all forms of communication are the hallmarks of those ruled by Mercury. Gemini is clever and quick with imagination and charm. They have a perpetual youthful appearance and positive outlook in life. Although restless and impatient, Gemini has an important role as a facilitator of knowledge and information. Gemini, the sign of brotherhood, is a messenger that really gets around and is a friend to everyone he meets.

CANCER

With the advent of the summer solstice, in the middle of a warm night, I look up and see that the Moon is following me. Ever-changing yet constant and follower of all, this ball of reflected light is a luminous sight. Like a mother always near, the Moon companion serves as a curiosity with universal appeal.

Cancer, the fourth sign of the zodiac, is ruled by the Moon. Cancer has associations to motherhood, family and home. The most sensitive and caring of all the signs, this emotional water sign has as its symbol the hard-shelled crab. With a tough exterior but gentle heart, the crab seeks to protect its deepest feelings of apprehension and vulnerability.

23

Cancer is intuitive, considerate and courteous with a strong maternal instinct and is inclined to be protective of friends and loved ones.

Like the many phases of the Moon, Cancer is thought to have many moods. They do not judge others and like the Moon, they prefer to gather, absorb and reflect. Basically quiet and shy, Cancer is slow to warm up to strangers. This is the sign of the regular Joe, a "people-person" who likes people and likes to share their life with others. Even though Cancer has the qualities for leadership, they favor the role of side-kick and find joy in doing whatever it is that "you're doing." More independent types find this trait somewhat clingy or smothering. But, Cancer is the sign that will be by your side when things get difficult in life and you need a trusting friend.

A childlike fascination with wonderland, the Cancer personality loves balloons and parties and make-believe. They have a vast imagination and would be happiest working in a creative endeavor. A believer in fantasy, anything shiny and bright attracts them. Also fond of the old and familiar, Cancer has a particular affection for children, babies and small animals. A patient soul with a gentle nature, the understanding Cancer secretly enjoys attention.

Cancer is the most private sign of the zodiac with a weakness to be fearful and pessimistic. The crab is cautious, not impulsive and will calculate their actions. Many times, Cancer the crab will walk sideways before proceeding forward. Security, emotionally and financially, is uppermost on the agenda of Cancer. They are often good with money because they realize that it helps provide security. Those born under the sign of Cancer show great tenacity with their personal possessions. Often frugal or parsimonious, those ruled by the Moon can have a distorted value system that elevates an old photograph or love letter to that of a treasured item.

Cancer craves affection and with their natural emotional insecurity, they need to hear you say you love them. They thrive on hugs and kisses. Sentimental and unselfish, Cancer is of hardy stock that can live to be quite old. This is someone who will bend over backwards for a person in need, and put those needs ahead of their own.

The basic nature of Cancer is sweet, diplomatic and polite. This chaser of moonbeams loves their home and has a deep sense of responsibility toward others. Sometimes a worrier, they can provide great companionship as a friend or as a lover in life. The crab may be elusive and like to hide on occasion, but never doubt the reliability of the one who will always be there for you in your time of need.

25

LEO

As the months go by, the seasonal development matures and the summer's rays turn the flower into fruit as it grows on the vine. Leo is the dawn of the ego, the ruler of us all. Psychologists say our ego and personality is completely formed by the time we are 5 years old, and so it is that in the fifth astrological allocation of time, life is full and round, settled and complete. This is a fire sign with all the warmth and love for life that exists. Ruled by the Sun, Leo is larger than life; it is life! Leos are generous, confident, strong and dignified.

To be yourself and express yourself, this is the kingdom of Leo. Power becomes them, whether they choose it or not. With a naturally noble character, Leo can be offended when not treated with honor and respect. Like its ruler the Sun, the largest and most dominant force in the zodiac, Leo represents creativity and originality, along with fatherhood, children and love. By nature of its symbol, the lion denotes majesty, integrity and wisdom.

Being one of the "fixed" signs in Astrology, Leo achieves results through persistence and determination. The positive attributes of fixed signs are constancy and reliability. Their movements and speech are deliberate. Leo usually means what they say and their trademark theme is, "I can do it myself." Leo finds it difficult to accept advice or financial help from others.

With Leo, there are two kinds of cats; the shy, quiet type and the flashy, flamboyant type. Deep down, all Leos are dramatic and have a colorful personality. There is a certain arrogant pride about them with a sunny playfulness at the same time. Leo is very proud and wants people to think well of them. The lion is very sophisticated, a superb organizer and always lovable.

Leo likes the good life. They like to live life to the fullest and go first class all the way. Leo makes an excellent host and will provide their guests with great food, wine and music. Seldom cautious with cash, Leo can be quite extravagant with spending money on fun and pleasure. This happy spirit rarely does anything halfway.

Leo rules the heart, and romance is more often on their minds than not. There are few bachelors or unmarried women born under the sign of Leo. They are very romantic and care a great deal about love and creating a family. But, keep in mind their naturally warm, affectionate nature can become disillusioned and disenchanted if they have difficulty finding true love or a soul mate.

A sometimes lazy cat, this natural leader is sympathetic and kind. The showy Leo who stands tall is usually adorned in beautiful attire. Leo is a loyal friend with true courage in their heart.

Leo shines best when in a position of authority and responsibility. The lion likes to work hard and play hard. Their royal manner has a stateliness that suits them. Leo will roll and bask in the warmth of compliments as their secret weakness is vanity. If people don't respect their wisdom and generosity or if they feel wounded, you may hear the roar of the lion; but as the saying goes, his roar is worse than his bite.

VIRGO

At the end of August when the Sun is a little lower in the sky, the Earth has become nice and warm and we begin the harvest season, a time of work and the astrological sign of Virgo. Virgo is the sign of work and interestingly an Earth sign, when our attentions turn to the season of harvesting from the soil. Earth signs are practical and dependable. This is a serious sign that is known for resourcefulness, skill in labor and an emphasis on getting the job done. Duty in service with an attention to detail, Virgo is industrious and not one to waste time. Virgos like truth, economy, prudence, and discrete selectivity.

Mercury, ruler of Virgo, is the closest planet to the Sun and revolves around the Sun at a feverish pace. While Mercury is associated with intelligence and communication, the sign Virgo is also a caring type. Those born under the sign of Virgo are prompted in life to serve or help others. Virgo sees a need and takes action as a facilitator to serve the need. Virgos are well suited to careers related to service.

Occupation is a word that literally means to occupy time, which works well to describe Virgo because Virgo is a nervous, energetic type with a great propensity for keeping busy. Virgos like to be productive and to make best use of time. Their mercurial talents make them good with note-taking, keeping a ledger, diary or log. They desire to bring order out of confusion. With a meticulous eye, Virgo has an appreciation for neatness and likes to do things properly and efficiently. Virgo is also methodical and discriminating. These traits make them excellent editors, secretaries, nurses and personal assistants.

Due to a restless nature, Virgo finds it difficult to relax, and most often is incapable of sitting still for any length of time. "The maiden," symbol for Virgo, is the incarnation of an all-natural being, choosing to live a pure and natural existence. When Virgo is not working, they enjoy keeping busy by reading or talking on the phone. In this way they can escape their ongoing concern with problems that weigh on their mind. Even though Virgo presents a tranquil expression, they are privately worried about something most of the time.

Virgo has a strong interest in diet and health. Their own delicate nervous system could benefit from daily exercise and a healthy menu plan. Virgos are not really exercise enthusiasts but being the "people-persons" that they are, perhaps walking with a friend could be just the ticket. Those born in September are concerned with cleanliness and you may notice a Virgo will always wash their hands before a meal. Virgo's studious personality and interest in learning enables them to succeed in many areas such as nutrition or other health related fields.

Prudence in love and money can be descriptive of the sign Virgo. In affairs of the heart, Virgo may have trouble finding a mate that measures up to their exacting standards of perfection. When married with a family, the Virgo spouse can bring stability and order to a household, which in turn provides a stable home for raising children.

Virgo is fastidious in grooming and conservative in their dress and appearance. They have no patience for laziness and are annoyed by vulgarity, stupidity, and carelessness. Negative traits for Virgo include inner anxieties and an exacting personality. Where Virgo seeks to analyze life to a perfecting degree, they often suffer from worry with the possibility of exhaustion from overworking. Virgo can be overly critical of others and have a narrow outlook on life.

Always the careful examiner and with clarity of thought, Virgo tends to be a cool, quiet type. Capable of self-denial, Virgo is one to give service to others but it is hard for them to accept favors from someone else. This mutable sign of Virgo is adaptable and flexible. They can go with the flow and take pleasure melding into the circumstances of the day.

LIBRA

As the planet Venus rules Libra and beauty, we see at the end of September and in October, nature's beauty in the extraordinary colors of the fall leaves. The colors range from yellow to orange to red and purple. Libra is positioned at the fall equinox and this time of year enjoys a balanced length of days and nights. The temperatures are neither hot nor cold, also balanced and representative of Libra's symbol, the scales.

Libra is the sign of love, partners and relationships. Any time two people have to get along and work together, they must strike a balance between them in order for the combined effort

35

to be successful. The harmony needed for two people to work together is the theme of Libra. The root word of relationship is relate.

Naturally popular, Libra is the greatest of all the signs designated as "people-persons." Their relationships to other people rank as the highest of priorities in their life. Libra considers the opinion of others to be of great value to them. This time of year is also known as "the season" for all things social, especially in fashion, art and the theater. To make a name for yourself, to become known, to be somebody, is often thought to be the end goal in Venusian associated careers. Whereas the opposite sign of Aries wants "to be me," Libra wants "to be somebody."

Always conscious of appearances, Libra is interested in hair, make-up, jewelry, and high fashion. A Libran has excellent manners, charm and grace. With keen social awareness, they behave in a dignified and polite way. The pleasant and good-natured Libran hates rudeness and is disturbed by displays of anger in private or in public.

Libra is an air sign which indicates an intellectual inclination. Librans seeks mental stimulation through communication and social interactions. They make friends easily and are interested in society, psychology and human relationships. Librans like to help people with their personal problems and therefore make very good counselors.

Libra has a special talent as a mediator or peacemaker. They have great success in getting opposing sides to work together. Known for harmony and balance, Libra has a tendency to weigh issues back and forth, making just comparisons for a fair outcome. In his own way, he is seeking out the truth, which is his true motive.

Despite their agreeable personalities and peacemaking abilities, it must be noted that Libra can be argumentative and suffer from indecisiveness. Libra appreciates a good debate, but after expressing one opinion, he may abruptly switch around and argue for the opposite side. A Libran has a profound ability for seeing both sides of a topic and likes to take all possibilities into consideration. Libra does not like to be hurried and dislikes making hasty decisions.

A romantic and lover of sweets, the sophisticated Libran is an artistic type, with a decided preference for culture and the finer things in life. Libra adores music, poetry, and art. They are a loving type with a generous heart for their friends and everyone in their circle.

SCORPIO

The wind spreads the last of the season's gifts of toil: the seed. The seed, a complete packet, packaged for tomorrow and ready for life when the conditions come together to serve Mother Nature's purpose, to continue life into the future. The seed represents eternity, the end and the beginning, and the circle of life. That is power and Scorpio is associated with unparalleled power in life.

Conception and death are the most outstanding issues associated with Pluto, ruler of the sign Scorpio. The miracle of conception is not just an expression; it represents a unique individual with a set of chromosomes like no one else on the Earth, that came into being at the moment of conception. Mother Nature is intent to reproduce, to make life continue. In fact, that is all she cares about and this sets up the natural nature of Scorpio, one that lives to succeed.

As a fixed sign, Scorpio accomplishes goals through a determined and persistent effort, often over an extended period of time. Those born in November, or late October, have tremendous staying power and will see any matter through to the end. The matters that Scorpio chooses to associate with are usually of serious consequence. Scorpio is very ambitious and has no fear. With an intense drive to investigate the nature of things, you may find them employed in professions associated with research, detection, biology or medicine. But, then again Scorpio is a sign that is not flavored by anything, due to its ruler Pluto, which is classed along with Mercury as a neutral body. So, in reality you could find a Scorpio in any job under the Sun.

Scorpio is a water sign that is sensitive to the feelings of others and has a strong intuitive power. They are non-aggressive types and accept life for what it is. Scorpio makes no attempt to present themselves in any way other than their natural self. They're not soft or naïve; if you ask their opinion or advice, you will get the naked, brutal truth. Scorpio is not always diplomatic since they believe in expressing their ideas and feelings with unfiltered truthfulness. They would rather remain silent than give a watered down version of their true opinions or emotions.

Those born under the sign of Scorpio like to travel incognito. You will rarely see them grinning or blushing; they prefer to keep their reactions to a minimum. Their composure is well-controlled with total ego. The secretive Scorpio likes to relentlessly probe your nature and motives, while remaining inscrutable themselves. Poised and calm, Scorpio wears a disguise of controlled reserve that hides their ongoing intense desire to win.

Scorpio never deals with life superficially and that is also true when it comes to their romantic involvements. The dark, magical, mysterious power of Pluto is responsible for the legendary passion of Scorpio. Their penetrating eyes and strong aura of personal magnetism help turn the heads of those they seek in the direction of their gaze. With a cool, careful and fixed intent, Scorpio pursues the object of their desire. When their affections turn serious, the vital force of Scorpio is always dedicated to the ties of family and love, and they are fiercely possessive of what they believe to be theirs.

Scorpio is sweet-natured and feels strongly about everything. They will always remember a gift or kindness and never forget an injustice. The life of a Scorpio is a constant struggle to conquer desire through creative use of the will, and like a seed, is a tightly packed container of potential.

SAGITTARIUS

In late November, the growing season has reached a close and the root cellar and pantry are brimming with nature's bounty. Sagittarius is the time of year that celebrates "joy" and "good will toward men." Under the rulership of Jupiter, it's a spiritual time associated with religion and philosophical thought. The benevolent sign of Sagittarius seeks to display leadership and achieves results through the power of positive thinking. Its symbol is the arrow that aims high toward lofty goals associated with higher thought, in fields such as education, mathematics and science. Sagittarius represents the intellectual ascent of man who has developed the capacity to think abstractly.

43

A fire sign that is known for enthusiasm, Sagittarius is naturally outgoing and energetic. Independent by nature they are extroverted and talkative. Those ruled by the centaur are highly civilized with good manners. They have high morals and proper etiquette. The sophisticated Sagittarius is usually dressed in designer clothing, and comfortable in any social setting with wit and intelligence.

Through association to Jupiter, Sagittarius is optimistic, idealistic and honest. This is an upbeat, positive sign known for straightforward frankness and blunt speech. Sagittarius wouldn't dream of hurting someone's feelings but sometimes they do quite innocently. They are free of malice and incapable of telling a lie.

Sagittarius is inherently restless and high strung. They have difficulty being still for long periods of time. Occasionally gregarious, Sagittarius does not take a subtle approach to life. Sagittarius has a great love of the outdoors, and for games and sports. They are more often found playing sports that involve the use of a club or racket as opposed to the use of pure muscles as in football or wrestling. With all their exuberance, Sagittarius can suffer from a propensity for being extra high or extra low. It is true that no one can be happier than a Sagittarius and at times, no one can be sadder. Sagittarius has a special affiliation for music, the conveyor of emotion in song.

With their natural love of life, Sagittarius loves love, like no other sign. More often, they are the pursuer, and aim their arrow straight for their intended's heart. Sagittarius is happiest when they are involved in a romantic relationship. However, they can be the victim of a broken heart because of their tendency to trust another too fast and too easily. When the time comes to settle down, Sagittarius may balk at the thought of marriage because they cherish their freedom and dislike confinement in any way. Once married though, Sagittarius will greatly enjoy family life with all that it entails, with children and pets and life's adventures.

An ongoing desire to make people happy, makes Sagittarius the comedian of the zodiac. This jovial soul can be quite entertaining and funny. Charming with a pleasant disposition, Sagittarius has a big heart, is patriotic and brave. Sometimes judgmental or naive, the easy-going Sagittarius endeavors to make the most of life. The archer is an idea person who is adaptable, flexible, and always ready to help their fellow man.

Sagittarius is high-class and enjoys the better things that life has to offer. They set high standards for themselves and live their life, like they are really going somewhere. The world is a better place with the wisdom, refinement and decorum displayed by those born in the sign of Sagittarius.

CAPRICORN

As we continue our seasonal trip through the zodiac, we come to Capricorn which begins on December 21, the winter solstice. Capricorn is marked by a dramatic loss of sunlight; it's the "dead of winter" and there is no evidence of life on the ground or in the environment. It's no wonder Capricorn is associated with coldness, melancholy and worry.

Capricorn is an earth sign which denotes practicality and sensibility. The strength of this sign is found in their ability to manage materials that allow for the necessities of life to continue. Capricorn rules self-autonomy; it is the most serious sign of the zodiac and the natives are known for their resourcefulness and organizational skills.

As a cardinal sign, Capricorn is identified with constructive initiative. It is the sign of livelihoods and burdens, and Capricorn has an inborn desire to accomplish something. Capricorn is tough-minded in business and often found in occupations associated with banking, law or the government. They have a great need to advance themselves and are likely to be in positions of authority and responsibility. Capricorn is quiet and ambitious, and like their symbol the mountain goat, they achieve success through a slow and steady ascent to the top of the mountain. Capricorn has an extreme capacity for hard work, and an inherent desire to advance their status in life.

Capricorn is ruled by the planet Saturn which is associated with the milestones of life, wisdom and maturity. The Saturnian personality has a sober temperament with a greater sense of duty than most people. Capricorns are not flashy and prefer to keep to their own affairs.

Saturn rules money and accumulated wealth. There is an interesting dichotomy in that Saturn governs wealth and poverty, sanitation and uncleanliness, capital and loss, along with gold and dirt. Capricorns are generally frugal types with a leaning toward being parsimonious.

As a rule, those born under Capricorn are a safe person to trust and in someone you can confide. Capricorn represents old school and the establishment with a respect for the laws and rules of life. They have old-fashioned values; they honor tradition and respect their elders. Capricorn also has a genuine interest in their ancestors and family history.

Dependable and reliable, Capricorn is actually a social climber, one who will make the most of opportunities that become available in their upward climb to the top. They are self-disciplined and serious about getting ahead. With amazing endurance, Capricorn will suffer and toil to attain success that will insure financial security, their ultimate goal. Often their negative traits like fear of uncertainty and a pessimistic view of life help propel them forward in their workplace efforts. The persistent Capricorn can be relentless in their desire to attain their sought after level of prosperity.

Despite appearing to be stern and gloomy, in truth, Capricorn is kindly and has a sensitive personality. They take pride in being humble and are really very private people. Capricorn lives life solemnly and most assuredly never wants to be dependent on others for subsistence.

The calm and responsible Capricorn has a head for business and excels in management. They may be stubborn at times, but basically they are a sweet soul. Their desire for self-preservation wins out, and the sturdy and solid Capricorn with his deliberate actions lives to be quite old, and is the final winner in the game of life.

AQUARIUS

In late January and February, the seasonal development that defines Aquarius is that the Sun has begun to return in the early evening hours. It is uplifting and brings an unexpected newness into our winter cold world. It is what you might call the very beginning of the next new year. Ruled by Uranus, the planet of change, Uranus pushes you away from darkness and into the light. White light is made up of all the colors of the rainbow and a rainbow, refreshing and renewing, is one of the symbols of Aquarius.

Another symbol for Aquarius is the lightening bolt. You may notice the shock of static electricity resulting from winter's lack of humidity at this time of year. February is noted for having unpredictable weather and atmospheric turbulence. And so it is, that Aquarius is the sign of wild and exciting weather; and stimulating people who serve a need to remove boredom from the world. Known for their individuality and unconventionality, Aquarius is a real live wire who can suddenly short circuit you with their amazing statements and actions.

Aquarius is an air sign indicating that they relate to others on a mental level. In social relationships, they have an impersonal nature and will give their opinion frankly. Those born in Aquarius think for themselves and usually do not change their views, regardless of public opinion. They are aloof, confident and usually at the head of the pack. They are coolly objective and rock star status fits them comfortably. Aquarius people are naturally charismatic; people are drawn to them, they look up to them and respect them.

Aquarius has a love of freedom, is idealistic and looks to the future. They have a universal concern for the well-being of mankind. Some keywords associated with this sign are humanitarianism, brotherhood, and fraternity. Aquarius governs "groups that work together," exemplifying the power of a gathering of like-minded people, to do good for the benefit of a community. This sign, of many friends, can be found in politics, spear-heading social reform or roaming the world on a mission of peace.

Original and creative, Aquarius is the sign associated with meteorology, chemistry and science. With their sharp perception and inclination to insist on "only the facts," Aquarius enjoys analyzing data and investigative study. "The hard truth" and "reality" are identified with its ruling planet, Uranus. Aquarius has a natural tendency toward inventiveness and thrives on diversity and novelty.

With an outward appearance of calmness, Aquarius is more likely to be keyed-up with an abundance of nervous energy. Some have eccentric temperaments that can produce unexpected eye-opening behaviors. Aquarius can display a bare minimum of tact and secretly enjoy shocking their acquaintances or friends. Negative traits include stubbornness, rigidity and a desire to control others.

Be prepared for the unexpected if someone you know was born in February when the daffy daffodils are coming up through the snow. Aquarius is a natural rebel with a universal mindset that everyone needs a good jolt in their life, and that they're just the one to deliver it!

PISCES

..."a pause in the day's occupations, that is known as the Children's Hour"...(from H.W. Longfellow's poem) is ephemeral and indescribable; the true beauty of life makes itself known at the end of February and in March, the final sign in the solar calendar, Pisces. At this time of the year, the world is holding its breath in anticipation of something wonderful. You can't put your finger on it, it's an idea, an illusive intuition. There's an intangible feeling that something is about to happen. You can't see it or hear it, but the signs are there and only those with a special perception can grasp it. Pisces is the season of inspiration and of hope.

A mutable water sign, Pisces is many things, but most of all it represents potential and talent. Everyone has talents, but it's the "tuning into" and the "paying attention to" that makes the difference between everyone else and Pisces.

Pisces is the sensitive one, who is thoughtful and concerned with the feelings of others. As the last sign of the zodiac, Pisces represents the maturity of civilization, that which embodies the idea of empathy. This is a blessing and a burden at the same time. Pisces often show more concern for another person's needs than for their own. In the big picture of life, Pisces is meant to serve mankind and his fellow human in some capacity.

Pisces has the ability to accept the imperfections of life, better than any of the other signs. There is a uniqueness to Pisces in that they have an understanding of the entire spectrum of humanity. It's a very personal sign, and one of their greatest natural abilities, is being kind to their fellow man. Those born in Pisces prefer to live in a gentle world where there is calmness and tranquility. Pisces suffer when exposed to harshness or conflict. They most definitely need to protect themselves from the abrasiveness of life.

Pisces may be a dreamer who doesn't make the best use of time, or he can harness his talents and rise above the frustrations that beset us all and become a great success in any field of his choosing. If Pisces has the fortitude to insulate themselves from the trauma of life, they can pursue their artistic inclinations, that come so naturally to them. This is the sign of creativity, expressed in art, music or poetry. Theater has an especially strong pull on Pisces, as it allows them to disguise themselves and live in a world of make-believe. Many teachers are born under the sign of Pisces because they care about children and are unselfish, endearing and devoted.

Neptune is the ruler of Pisces and is symbolized by two fish swimming in opposite directions. This is said to indicate a temperament that can vary back and forth, from strongly optimistic to acutely pessimistic. Neptune is associated with all things "water" including lakes, oceans, mist, or fog. Things that are unclear like clouds, gases, misconceptions, and mysteries, come under the heading of things ruled by Neptune, along with confusion, bliss and love.

The Pisces personality has a need for privacy and can be timid, indecisive, and easily influenced. Pisces does not have strong will-power. They may lack ambition or motivation and will often take the path of least resistance. Pisces hasn't any particular desire for power or wealth. The reserved Pisces may have health issues and find it necessary to conserve energy and take especially good care of themselves.

Pisces stands back from the world as a guru with highly developed senses, versatility and wisdom. They are altruistic and have an antenna that is geared to the softer side of life. Look for the illusive Pisces hiding in the serene waters of life. You'll find them lending a hand to another who will benefit immensely from the one with charity in their heart.

MAGNETIC ATTRACTION

Magnetic attraction is the force felt between two "unlike" poles of a magnet. And, *magnetic repulsion* is the force felt between two "like" poles of a magnet. By applying this scientific information to the twelve zodiac signs that have each been given a polarity designation, you have the "compatibility theory of the plus / minus," which is "opposites attract." The cover of this book shows the "togetherness" of the attracted unlike poles and the back cover shows the "separation" or repulsion of the magnet's poles of the same polarity. "...there is a distance between us..." is a literal description.

59

Magnetic attraction is defined as an attraction for iron, associated with electrical currents as well as magnets; characterized by fields of force. Attractive force is the force by which one object attracts another.

The poles of a magnet are points where their magnetic strength is concentrated. These points are labeled north and south because suspended magnets will orient along the north-south planes of the Earth. Magnetism is involved in almost everything we do, yet no one really thinks about it.

Basic science tells us that magnetism is the force of attraction or repulsion between substances made of certain materials, such as iron, nickel, cobalt, and steel. This force of magnetism is actually due to the motion of electric charges which is going on, all the time, on an elemental level.

All electricity is made from magnets. When a magnet is spun inside a coil of wire, electrons start to flow from the wire. Power plants use fuel to spin magnets to make electricity.

The Earth is a giant magnet and there are liquid metals deep inside the earth that create convection currents which in turn create magnetic force. Scientists believe that the magnetic force surrounding the Earth makes life possible and that without the "magnetic force field," too much energy would reach the Earth from the Sun and our atmosphere would be eliminated.

All animals, humans included, have small magnetite crystals in their brains. It is believed that animals may navigate or migrate by sensing the pull of the magnetite crystals toward the Earth's magnetic poles.

MECHANICS OF PLUS / MINUS

All matter in the world and the universe, whether animate or inanimate, is made up of atoms. These fundamental building blocks of matter contain particles that have the property of being electrically charged, either positive, negative or neutral. This electrical component is manifest as protons, electrons or neutrons. And as such, a "plus and minus phenomenon" exists and is present in everything in our known world.

There are four fundamental Forces of Nature. Gravity is a force that acts between any two objects with mass in the universe and it has infinite range. The second force called electromagnetism acts between electrically charged particles. Electricity, magnetism and light are all produced by this force, and it has infinite range.

The third force is called the strong force and it binds neutrons and protons together in the cores of atoms and is a short range force. The fourth force is called the weak force. This force causes beta decay (the conversion of a neutron to a proton, an electron and an anti-neutrino); various particles are formed by strong interactions, but decay via weak interactions. Like the strong force, the weak force is short range. Without these fundamental forces, all matter in the universe would fall apart and float away.

The dictionary defines a magnet as a material or object that produces a magnetic field. A magnetic field is *invisible*, but it is responsible for the most notable property of a magnet: a force that pulls on ferromagnetic materials, such as iron, and attracts or repels other magnets. A bar magnet or the familiar horseshoe shaped magnet is marked with an S and an N to designate its poles, S for "South" and N for "North." Two poles of the same charge (S & S or N & N) will repel each other. One of each pole (S & N) will display an attraction to each other.

64

The Earth itself is scientifically defined as a gigantic magnet with the North Pole at one end and the South Pole at the other end of an invisible axis that runs through the center of the Earth.

An electric motor works because of the fundamental property of magnetic repulsion between "like poles" or (S & S) and (N & N) charges. All our appliances, cars and computers depend on this force that is found in science / nature.

The forces of nature are all around. Our own brain is an electrical and chemical machine with tiny brain cells called neurons that shoot electrical impulses down a "wire" (an axon) in an off and on manner. All these billions of axons generate an amount of electrical charge, estimated to equal the power of a 60 watt light bulb.

Science lays out the laws of nature and Astrology has applied this information to its basic set of designations for the twelve signs of the zodiac. The plus / minus theory of compatibility in this book is simply making good use of something that already exists and is present in everything in our world.

The referencing of each of the Astrology signs as being either positively charged or negatively charged is not new. It has always been around since Astrology first began. And to my knowledge, no one has ever used the polarity designation as a basis for compatibility. But, once realized it is easily understood. A love relationship between two people must have one positive sign and one negative sign for the mechanics of the relationship to work.

When a plus and a minus do get together, a climate for love has been created. There is no friction between them. They work together instead of against each other. This is a combination that is needed for any growth or continuance to occur, to be fruitful or produce happiness.

In nature, two positives (males) cannot mate and reproduce, and 2 negatives (females) cannot mate and reproduce. The plus / minus theory of compatibility is Mother Nature's law, the law of all living things.

COMPATIBILITY

This book is about love, human compatibility and marriage. It's been said that the most important decision you will ever make is the decision you make to marry. Current statistics tell us that the success rate for marriage is 50/50. That doesn't sound like very good odds, and this fact alone could influence someone not to marry.

This manuscript about "love compatibility" interprets the little known and overlooked fact from Astrology that says each of the twelve signs has a "polarity designation" of either positive or negative. The theory presented here seeks to make known the

67

importance of this seemingly small detail. This information is intended to give someone an invaluable tool that will increase one's chances to marry successfully and in so doing achieve greater success and happiness in life.

How could people be so bad at picking out a future life partner? One reason so many people end up mismatched is because people seek someone that is like themselves. It's perfectly natural that two people would be drawn to each other through similarities. Regarding polarity, you are either a plus or you are a minus. "Plus" sign people think alike and "minus" sign people think alike. Sometimes, this likeness can be mistaken for love.

When we are young and looking for a mate, we likely give the greatest consideration in our selection to physical attractiveness and looks. This singular selection approach creates a randomness that suggests that it will be pure luck or chance that we end up with the correct polarity. We can take some solace in the fact that a certain number of people have a natural instinct about compatibility and match well because of it.

Obviously, there is an unlimited number of personality traits that all people possess, far too many traits to review when discussing the matching-up of two people. Our theory here only concerns itself with a base starting point, which should come first before any other considerations. A relationship needs one positive and one negative to make a match. Think of this as a foundation for building a relationship, not unlike the foundation for building a house. Both involve your future and may last a lifetime.

There is hardly any area of one's life that isn't touched by the benefits or detriment of a relationship that works or doesn't work. When people aren't happy, their worst side comes out. When two people in a relationship are misaligned as in two "plus signs" or two "minus signs," there can be a constant undercurrent of stress, a tide that has to be fought against. It is a subtle influence and difficult to pinpoint or define. It's there and no one can figure out what the heck is wrong or why they suddenly are not so much in love any more. More times than not, each person in a faulty relationship thinks that the problem lies with the other person, that there is something "wrong" with their spouse or significant other.

Concerning love relationships, it's important to know that just because you have the plus / minus designation correct, it does not mean that you are with a person that is compatible to you. This is critical information and is equally as important as the original premise that states, you need one "plus sign" and one "minus sign" for a compatible match.

As far as dating is concerned, the plus / minus should be thought of as "that person is a possibility" or "that person is not a possibility." When you are "out there" in the dating scene, a person should always use their natural instincts and good judgment to be safe when meeting new people. Meet at a public location and tell someone where you will be.

In a love relationship, balance can be experienced if each of the persons are of a different polarity. There is a natural equilibrium that occurs when a plus and a minus join together and this makes a working relationship. A special beam of love and happiness can happen between two people with the correct polarity. In time, this joy can be passed on to their children. Two pluses or two minuses can never make a circle. Only one plus and one minus, together, can make a circle of love and a circle of life.

LOVE AND SEX

Try to put two magnets together that are of the same polarity;
you are unable to force them together. But the opposite poles
attract like crazy and you can't keep them apart. Touching may
be the single most important attribute reflective of love itself.
Touch is love, the attraction is in the physical sense of touch.

Human life could not exist or continue without the coming
together of two people. Sex between a man and a woman is
Mother Nature's most simplistic expression of the plus / minus
phenomenon in life. In the animal kingdom, the idea of one
male and one female represents one plus and one minus.

71

Plumbers use the adjectives "female" and "male" to describe components when referring to the joining of pipes. It is clear that two female parts cannot conjoin to one another and that two male parts cannot fit together. Not unlike sex, this mimics the building block of life. It takes two to fit together and those two have to be different, one male and one female for it to work. Funny how incompatible couples always use the expression, "we couldn't make it work."

Sensuality is always at the forefront of any healthy and happy love relationship. Love is a physical attraction with an unexplainable emotional response. It's an undercurrent that sweeps between two people who have a successful sex life. There's sex and then there's love sex.

The objective of this book is to help men and women become aware of the "plus / minus phenomenon" that Astrology lays out, in order to help them select the correct partner for their love and sex life. Sex is difficult enough without having to navigate with someone who is magnetically incompatible to you.

The electrical component of either a positive force or a negative force effectively reveals that two of the same polarity will physically repel each other, resulting in conflict. On the other hand, two complimentary poles, each with a different force will be drawn together allowing for the development of a special bond to occur between two people.

If two positive poles are in a relationship or if two negative poles are in a relationship, the romance may be of a cool nature. One may have a feeling that the relationship is somehow challenged or problematic.

Love and sex are areas of life in which, if two people have the right connection, their sex life can grow and continually improve as two people spend their lives together. The quality of your sex life will be in direct relation to the amount of time and effort that you put into it. Intimacy can happen when persons are of unlike polarities.

Chances of finding a special love may come to you by chance or destiny. For the rest of us, better keep track of someone you date's Astrology sign. You have little chance of great love if you hook up with the wrong polarity. In some instances, Mother Nature plays tricks on us and makes us attracted to the wrong sign.

People in non-compatible relationships may rationalize that the bedroom is the only problem between them and that they are very compatible in most everything else.

Love is all about caring about the needs of someone else. It is possible to love someone of a like pole. There is no way that anyone could imagine that this technical phenomenon exists between people; so those in an incompatible relationship press forward and make life happen regardless of the challenges that it presents.

I don't know of any Astrology publication that has recognized that the polarity of the 12 birth signs should be considered a determining factor in compatibility. The theory in this book says that each person is only compatible with 6 or less Astrology signs. For this reason, our goals for finding love, our preconceived ideas and ideals for that perfect partner need to be scaled back. Many times, couples with really great relationships came upon it quite by accident. In order to find someone with the correct polarity we need to expand our thinking as to who we consider an eligible single to date.

MISMATCHED

The expression, mismatched, is used in this book to describe a couple in which both parties have the same polarity; Aries and Gemini, for instance.

It is important to acknowledge, that there are a lot of people who are married to the wrong polarity and they have adapted to the conditions of their life. These are normal, proud, regular people who happened to have married the wrong sign and they have adjusted and made a life for themselves which happens to include an imperfect relationship with a spouse.

75

Most often, the mismatch of two people affects the relationship in the most personal of issues, the bedroom. To quote a line from a famous play written by Tennessee Williams, "If the marriage is on the rocks, the rocks are in the bed."

The human spirit to live and be happy doesn't give up easily and will find ways to cope with the terms of a mismatched combination. In the face of less than perfect situations, people rise up and carry on and can still do great things. Ironically, it becomes a great motivator to prove to others that things are OK.

In this crazy game called love, it turns out that when two people can't get along; it's nobody's fault, they're just not compatible. It's a very radical idea to think that two people who are married or who are a couple are actually not compatible. When two people get married, they usually share the same goals in life, namely to put down roots and have a family. Who could possibly imagine that the person they have selected to marry is "not compatible" to them?

The term dysfunctional has become a popular catch phrase and may be used to describe the outcome of a partnership that includes two positively charged signs or two negatively charged signs. In theory, this is an inadequate foundation for a relationship or for making a family. Of course, people do it

76

every day, marry the wrong polarity. Who would think in their wildest dreams that there could exist such a phenomenon, that indicates such a profound and exacting occurrence, that is described in this book? It seems ludicrous to suggest, that if your birthday is on a certain date and your romantic other's birthday is on a certain date, that you are or are not compatible.

The expression, "a personality conflict" is often used to account for unexplainable conflict between two people. After matrimony, you may find that you've made a grave error. If things go wrong, living conditions can get very unpleasant. Sometimes "the courts" start to run people's lives and tell them when they can and cannot see their *own children*. Monetary arrangements add more stress to the situation. All this trouble in life that may have stemmed from marrying the wrong sign.

I certainly wouldn't recommend breaking up any marriages or families. It is a fact that most people just stick it out rather than endure all that comes with divorce.

It is suspected that problems resulting from living in a mismatched union, cause much more trouble than one might realize. Mismatched people engage in negative behavior in order to cope. All the usual suspects include drinking, smoking, overeating or cheating come into play and any other self-endangering activity. These behaviors may appear to be the problem, when really they are just a symptom of the real problem.

After you marry someone of the same polarity, your ability to grow as a person may lessen. Growing is the most important feature of life because growth is life itself. You start to adapt to the situation. Depending on the particular issues between two people in a relationship, you may start to spend your time coping with living with the other person instead of spending your time developing yourself, and improving yourself along with living your life.

The majority of mismatched people learn to live in a side by side relationship as opposed to sharing a relationship. Most people who are mismatched have no idea why "things are so hard!" Perhaps you're overweight and no matter what you do, you cannot lose weight. Eating becomes your coping mechanism to survive what is wrong in your life.

Maybe you cannot sleep. That is your coping mechanism, forcing you to focus on yourself. You need comfort and attention because you have to try so hard every day to cope with something difficult that you are powerless to understand or change.

The basic situation is that you are incompatible with your spouse. Living with constant friction and disapproval can alter the way a person thinks about oneself. Happiness becomes illusive and many times a person thinks that there is something wrong with the mate or the other way around; the person thinks it is their fault and that they have to try harder to please their spouse.

The institution of marriage has many different meanings and many different customs around the world. Generally, people love the idea of getting married. It's romantic; some people "run off" and get married. There's a sense of permanency that is desirable and people somehow feel protected when they are "in a marriage."

Everyone marries with good intentions. It's a testament to the sincerity and goodness of a vast number of people who marry and are not compatible, but still put their best foot forward and do the right thing. It is also a fact that people will stay in a bad marriage and hang in there "for dear life" and not let go for any reason. Nobody wants to get divorced. In general, people will do anything to stay married.

IN CONCLUSION

"I believe that there is a subtle magnetism in Nature, which, if we unconsciously yield to it, will direct us aright." is a quote from Henry David Thoreau, American author, poet and philosopher.

To find compatibility we must follow the laws of nature by joining with another who is the opposite in polarity to ourselves. Ask any scientist and he will tell you that the phenomenon of the plus / minus is readily observed through the science of magnets and it is one of the basic forces of nature.

81

If we take away just one thing from Astrology, let it be this formula for compatibility in love and sex. This book claims that by choosing a mate that is the correct polarity for you, a person will achieve greater happiness, success and personal growth in life.

The age old strategy for staying together in marriage has always been for people to "tough it out." It was assumed that you needed to "try harder" to make it work. Well, this book proclaims that with two people of the same polarity in a marriage or union; it isn't working and it won't work, no matter how hard you try. This is a finite situation that will never change. It's not something that you can solve or work through.

This plus / minus theory of compatibility says that everyone is only compatible with the Astrology signs that are the opposite polarity to your own sign. This limits the number of possibilities for each person in their search for love. Every person is only compatible with 3, 4, 5 or 6 Astrology signs. You may have to consider that the best person for you isn't going to fit into a small category of people who are exactly like you, or fit a physical model of perfection that you are searching to find. The match for you will most likely be very different from you.

It's a fact that Astrology is still considered vital because the zodiac signs are listed in the client profiles on dating apps and websites. When you're in a compatible relationship, you have a built-in support system. You have someone in your corner when life gets challenging. You care for each other's welfare and are there for each other in times of stress. People in compatible relationships often say, "I married my best friend."

Even the best of relationships are not smooth all the time, but with this information you can significantly hedge your bet. The effort involved in finding someone that you are attracted to, who is also the right polarity, will be worth your time when the reward is a love sex relationship that represents mature love.

A brief description that explains the Chinese philosophy of yin-yang follows. This interestingly shares and somewhat aligns with the idea of the positive / negative forces presented here.

To quote from Wikipedia: "In Chinese philosophy, the concept of yin-yang, which is referred to in the west as "yin and yang," literally means "shadow and light" is used to describe how polar opposites or seemingly contrary forces are interconnected and interdependent in the natural world, and how they give rise to each other in turn in relation to each other. The concept lies at the origins of many branches of classical Chinese science and philosophy, as well as being a primary guideline of traditional Chinese medicine among other things. Many natural dualities – e.g., dark and light, female and male, low and high, cold and hot, water and fire, earth and air – are thought of as manifestations of yin and yang (respectively). Yin and yang are not opposing forces (dualities), but complimentary forces, unseen (hidden, feminine) and seen (manifest, masculine), that interact to form a greater whole, as part of a dynamic system. Everything has both yin and yang aspects as light could not be understood if darkness didn't exist, and shadow cannot exist without light."

So many people view Astrology under the heading of fantasy, but in reality, the planets have gravity and our universe is all one "matter and force-defined" world. Science and Mother Nature are the forces of life that Astrology seeks to define. Good advice maintains, don't sign any contracts with a person of the same polarity unless safeguards are in place for your future well-being.

The information in this book will set a new precedent as to who is compatible to whom. This plus / minus theory of compatibility reduces complicated forces of nature into a simple reference of plus and minus. Yin cannot exist without yang...how romantic!

FOR ASTROLOGERS

There are 3 considerations when advising a client about compatibility using Astrology. The first is to only consider the 6 signs of opposite polarity to the person's sign. If you have a birth time, you can also eliminate the opposite polarity signs that are found on the client's ascendant, nadir and moon sign. A person is not compatible with the signs that fall on their ascendant, nadir or moon sign. This determination sets which zodiac signs have potential compatibility for the client. Every person is only compatible to 3, 4, 5 or 6 signs.

The next two considerations involve the comparing of two charts for Fatal Flaws and Pressure Points. It is considered a Fatal Flaw and incompatible if any of these markers: sun, ascendant, nadir or moon are in the same sign as any of the markers in the other person's chart.

A Pressure Point is defined as an unfavorable angle (opposition, square or conjunction) at an exact degree that is found between the sun, moon, planets or critical positions (ascendant or nadir) in the charts of the 2 people being considered for compatibility. If the planets are malefic, these aspects can be responsible for incompatibility.

These conditions for compatibility are the ideal.

If there is no birth time, sunrise is most suitable to use, as the location of the moon and the planets at sunrise sets the horoscope for the day.

POLARITY CARD

Cut out and laminate:

North polarity (+)		South polarity (-)	
Aries	3/21 to 4/19	Taurus	4/20 to 5/20
Gemini	5/21 to 6/20	Cancer	6/21 to 7/22
Leo	7/23 to 8/22	Virgo	8/23 to 9/22
Libra	9/23 to 10/22	Scorpio	10/23 to 11/21
Sagittarius	11/22 to 12/21	Capricorn	12/22 to 1/19
Aquarius	1/20 to 2/18	Pisces	2/19 to 3/20